Presented to

_____

By

_____

On

_____

My First Bible
CATHOLIC EDITION

Edited by

Ruth Hannon
and
Rev. Victor Hoagland, C.P.

Illustrations by

J. Verleye

Cover Illustration by

George Angelini

THE REGINA PRESS
New York

IMPRIMATUR:

C. Eykens, vic gen.
Antverpiae, 31 Augustus 1991

THE REGINA PRESS
145 Sherwood Avenue
Farmingdale, New York 11735

ISBN: 0-88271-250-0

Cover illustration by George Angelini
Text designed and typeset by Roth Advertising

PRINTED IN BELGIUM

FOREWORD

This Bible is written especially for you: It tells in simple words all about God's love from the beginning of time. It teaches through delightful tales how faithful God has always been. As you read this Bible, you will also learn about Jesus and his teachings. You will read how Jesus and the Holy Spirit started the Church on the feast of Pentecost. And you will recognize the Holy Spirit who guides the Church today.

Reading the Bible will bring you closer to God. Before you begin, say the following prayer for understanding and grace.

PRAYER

Heavenly Father, grant me special grace to understand the message you have placed here for me. Thank you for being always faithful to your people—from the creation of the world up to today. May I learn from the example of your Son Jesus and may I grow daily in my love for you. Amen.

INTRODUCTION

The Bible has two parts, the Old Testament and the New Testament. The men who wrote these stories were inspired and guided by God, the Holy Spirit. That is why we say the Bible is the word of God.

We should read the Bible as often as we can. It tells how God made the world and every living thing and how his Son, Jesus, came to save us from evil and show us the way to Heaven.

It is the most important story in all the world.

THE OLD TESTAMENT

The first part of the Bible tells the story of Creation, the beginning of the world and our first parents. There are also many stories about the people God chose to bring us his message and to lead us.

All of this happened a very long time ago. No one knows exactly when because there were no such things as dates or calendars. Everything took place before the coming of Jesus.

TABLE OF CONTENTS

Old Testament

New Testament

Old
Testament

God Made the World

In the beginning God made the earth and the skies. And he gathered the waters of the earth together to make the seas. Then God said, "Let plants and trees grow upon the earth," and it was done. And God made the sun and the moon, and he filled the sky with stars. And he said, "Let the waters and skies be filled with living things, and let animals dwell upon the earth." And it came to pass as God had said.

And God made a man and a woman, and he saw that all he had done was good. In six days God made the world and on the seventh he rested.

Adam and Eve

The Lord God made Adam, the first man, and placed him in the Garden of Eden. And God told Adam that he might eat anything in the garden except the fruit of the tree of knowledge. Then God made a woman, Eve, and she was Adam's companion. But a serpent said to Eve, "God forbids you to eat that fruit because if you do, you will become like him." And Adam and Eve disobeyed God and ate that fruit.

God knew what they had done, and he said, "Because you have not obeyed me, you must leave this place." And Adam and Eve went out sadly from the beautiful Garden of Eden.

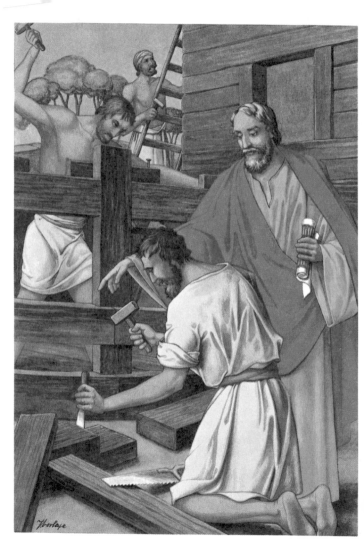

Noah's Ark

In time people grew so wicked that God said to Noah, "I shall send a flood, but you will be saved because you are a good man. Build an ark and take into it your family and two of every kind of animal." And Noah did as God commanded.

Then the rains fell for forty days and destroyed all living things except Noah and the others in the ark. When the storm was over, Noah set free a dove. But she did not return and Noah knew she had found a place to perch and that the waters had gone down. Then he and the others stepped forth on dry land.

God Calls Abram

The Lord said to Abram, "Leave your home and go to a land I will show you." And Abram went out of his house with Sara his wife and all he owned. When he came to Canaan, the Lord said, "I will give this land to you and to your family forever." And Abram and Sara dwelt in Canaan.

The Lord was pleased with Abram, and he said to him, "Your name will now be Abraham, and your wife's will be Sarah. And I will give you a son whom you will call Isaac."

When the obedient Abraham and Sarah had a son, they named him Isaac, as the Lord had commanded.

Jacob's Vision

Abraham's son Isaac was the father of Jacob. One night when Jacob was on a journey, he lay on the ground and slept. In a dream he saw a ladder that reached to heaven, and on it angels were going up and down. Then the Lord said to Jacob, "I am the God of Abraham and of Isaac. I will give to you and your children the land on which you are lying, and in your family the earth will be blessed."

When Jacob woke up, he said, "The Lord was here! This is the house of God and the gate of heaven." And he called that place Bethel.

Joseph and his Brothers

Jacob had many sons, but Joseph was the one he loved best. When Jacob made Joseph a fine coat, his brothers grew angry and planned to kill the boy. But they decided to sell him instead, and after they took away his coat, they sold him to some traders for twenty pieces of silver.

Then the brothers dipped the coat into animal blood and sent it to Jacob their father. And the old man cried, "This is the coat of my son. He has been killed by wild beasts."

But Joseph was alive, for the traders had sold him as a slave in the land of Egypt.

Joseph in Egypt

While Joseph was a slave in Egypt, Pharaoh, the King, sent for him and said, "I dreamt I saw seven fat cows, but seven thin cows ate them up. Then I saw seven fine ears of wheat, but seven thin ears swallowed them. What is the meaning of this dream?"

Joseph said, "God will send seven good years and then seven years when nothing will grow. In the good years let a wise man store food for people to eat in the bad years."

"You are wise, Joseph," said Pharaoh, "and I place this land in your care." And he gave Joseph a ring, and people bowed down to him.

Joseph Saves his Family

Joseph had enough wheat to feed all of Egypt in the bad years. But at home his father Jacob had no food, and he told his sons, "Go down to Egypt for wheat." When Joseph saw his brothers, he knew them at once, but none of them knew him.

They told him about their young brother Benjamin whom their father loved, and about Joseph who they said had died.

Then Joseph said, "I am your brother, and I forgive you for selling me to strangers. Bring my father to Egypt to live." And Jacob and his sons went to Egypt and there they made their homes.

The Baby Moses

In Egypt, Pharaoh ordered that all Israelite boy babies be killed. Now a certain Israelite woman had a son, and to save him she put him in a basket which she hid by the river. But his sister kept watch nearby.

When Pharaoh's daughter, a princess, came to the river, she picked up the baby and cried, "An Israelite child!" The baby's sister asked, "Shall I get an Israelite woman to nurse him?" "Yes," said the princess, and the girl fetched her mother who cared for the baby till he grew up. Then she took him to the princess who named him Moses.

The Burning Bush

While Moses guarded his sheep one day, he saw a bush that was on fire. He went up to it and heard the Lord calling, "Moses!" And Moses said, "Here I am." "Take your sandals from your feet," said the Lord, "you are on holy ground." And the Lord said, "Moses, I know how cruelly Pharaoh treats the Israelites. Tell him you will lead them out of Egypt."

"But I do not speak well," said Moses. "How can I talk to Pharaoh?" "Your brother Aaron is a good speaker," said the Lord. "Take him to Pharaoh, and I shall tell him what to say." And Moses did as the Lord commanded.

Moses and Aaron See Pharaoh

Moses went with his brother Aaron to Pharaoh and said, "The Lord commands you to let the Israelites go." But Pharaoh said, "No! They must stay here." The Lord then commanded Aaron to cast down his staff before Pharaoh. When he obeyed, the staff became a snake.

Pharaoh then commanded his wise men to do as Aaron had done, and each of their staffs also turned into a snake. But Aaron's staff swallowed all the others. Still Pharaoh would not let the Israelites go. But Moses knew the Lord would save his people.

Across the Red Sea

At last Pharaoh let the Israelites go, and Moses led them to the Red Sea. But Pharaoh changed his mind and sent his soldiers to bring the Israelites back. The people were frightened when they saw the soldiers, but God said to Moses, "Lift your staff over the sea. It will open and the people may walk across on dry land."

Moses obeyed and the people marched to the other shore. But the Egyptians followed them into the passage, and the Lord told Moses, "Stretch your staff over the sea again." The waters closed over the Egyptians, and all were drowned.

The Commandments

When the Israelites came to the desert of Sinai, they saw a mountain covered with clouds, and from its top a trumpet sounded loudly. Moses told the people to wait while he went up the mountain, and there the Lord told him how he expected his people to act. They were to tell the truth. They were to love God and honor their parents. They were to say God's name respectfully. They were not to steal or to hurt others. These were God's commandments.

The Lord wrote his commandments on two stone tablets and gave them to Moses to carry down to the people.

The Golden Calf

When Moses came down from the mountain, he saw the people dancing around a calf made of gold and worshiping it as their true God. This made Moses so angry that he threw down the stone tablets and broke them. "You have offended God," he cried. And he destroyed the golden calf.

Again Moses went up the mountain, and again God gave him stone tablets upon which he wrote the commandments. Moses stayed on Mount Sinai for forty days, talking with the Lord, and when he came down, his face shone so brightly that he had to cover it with a veil.

The Walls of Jericho

After Moses died, Joshua led the Israelites toward Jericho in Canaan. But around this city, a wall had been built to keep the Israelites out. Then the Lord said to Joshua, "Let the people march around Jericho once a day for six days. On the seventh day, let them march seven times. Then, when the priests blow on rams' horns, let all the people shout."

Joshua obeyed, and on the last day when the people marched around the city, the horns blew and everyone shouted. At once the walls fell, and the Israelites marched into the city, as God had promised.

Young David

The Lord said to Samuel, a prophet in Israel, "Go to Isai in Bethlehem, for I have chosen a king from among his sons. I will show you which one it is. Bless that boy with oil, and one day he will rule my people."

Samuel looked at seven sons of Isai, but the Lord said, "It is none of these." Then Samuel asked Isai, "Are these all the sons you have?" "No," said Isai, "my youngest is minding sheep," and Samuel said, "Bring him to me." This boy was named David, and the Lord said to Samuel, "David will be king. Bless him." And God was with David from that day.

David and Goliath

One morning David took food to his brothers who were in camp. There he heard about Goliath, an enemy soldier who each day called to the Israelites, "Send a man to fight me." But the Israelites were afraid, for Goliath was a giant. David said, "I will fight him and God will be with me." Carrying only a sling and five stones, he walked toward the enemy.

Goliath saw David and he ran at him, but the boy threw one of his stones and it struck Goliath in the forehead. When the giant fell, the enemy soldiers ran away, and the Israelites won the day.

Elias Is Fed by an Angel

Elias was a good and holy man, but because he was so good, a wicked queen wanted to harm him, and Elias had to run away.

After he had walked many days, he fell asleep under a tree, but an angel came and said, "Get up and eat." And Elias saw bread and a jar of water at his side. He ate and drank and fell asleep again. But once more the angel came and said, "Get up and eat and drink, for you have a long way to go." And again Elias ate and drank. The food was so good that Elias was able to walk for forty days without eating again.

Personal Record

Name_____
  born_____ **in**_____

Baptism
  Date_____
  Priest_____
  Parish_____
  Godfather_____
  Godmother_____

First Communion
  Date_____
  Priest_____
  Parish_____

Confirmation
  Date_____
  Bishop_____
  Parish_____
  Sponsor_____
  Confirmation name_____

Family Record

Father_____
    born_____in_____

Mother_____
    born_____in_____

Brothers and Sisters_____

_____

_____

Father's family
    Grandfather_____
        born_____
    Grandmother_____
        born_____

Mother's family
    Grandfather_____
        born_____
    Grandmother_____
        born_____

New
Testament

THE NEW TESTAMENT

The second part of the Bible is the story of Jesus, the Son of God, his birth, life, death and resurrection.

Everything Jesus did and all the truths he taught were so important that our biggest celebrations are now related to events in his life. For example, on Christmas day we celebrate the birth of Jesus, and on Easter Sunday we celebrate his rising from the dead.

Now that Jesus is in Heaven, he continues to help us by sending the Holy Spirit to fill our hearts with love and wisdom.

An Angel Speaks to Mary

In Nazareth there lived a young woman named Mary who was engaged to Joseph, a carpenter, and an angel of the Lord came to her with a message. "Do not be afraid, Mary," said the angel. "God has sent me to tell you that you will be the mother of a son, and his name will be Jesus."

Mary was surprised, but the angel said, "The Holy Spirit will come to you, and your child shall be called the Son of God. He shall rule a kingdom that will last forever."

And Mary said, "I am God's servant. I will do what he asks."

And the Angel went away.

Jesus is Born

In time Mary and Joseph, her husband, went to Bethlehem. But the town was crowded and they had to sleep in a cave. Mary's baby, Jesus, was born there that night.

Nearby an angel came to some shepherds who were watching their sheep, and he said, "A child has been born in Bethlehem. He is Christ the Lord." And many angels sang:

"Glory to God in the highest, And peace on earth."

The shepherds went to Bethlehem to see the child and they found him with Mary and Joseph. Then the shepherds went away praising God.

The Child Jesus in the Temple

After a holiday, Mary and Joseph were returning home to Nazareth with their friends and the twelve-year-old Jesus. At first Mary thought Jesus was with another family, but when she learned he was not, she and Joseph went back to Jerusalem to look for him. They searched for three days before they found him in the temple. He was talking with teachers who were amazed at his knowledge of God's teachings.

Mary asked, "Son, why have you worried us so?" Jesus answered, "Didn't you know that I must do my Father's work?" But he went home with Mary and Joseph and obeyed them.

The First Apostles

When Jesus was thirty years old, he set out to tell people about God's great love for them. One day, as he walked near the Sea of Galilee, he saw two brothers, Peter and Andrew. They were fishing with nets, but Jesus said to them, "Follow me." At once they left their work and went with him.

Further on he saw two other brothers, James and John, who were sitting in a boat with their father, mending nets. Jesus asked the brothers to follow him, and they, too, left their work and their father to follow Jesus.

A Marriage at Cana

When a marriage was held at Cana, Jesus was there with Mary, his mother. Soon all the wine was gone, and Mary said to Jesus, "There is no wine left." And he asked, "What can I do about it?" But Mary whispered to the waiters, "Do whatever my son commands you." Then Jesus told them, "Fill the tall jars with water and let the headwaiter taste it."

But the water had turned into wine, and after the headwaiter took a sip, he said, "It is the best wine we have served today." This was the first of the many wonderful things Jesus did.

Jesus Speaks to the People

One day Jesus went to a mountain top, and he spoke to the people. He said, "Love everyone, even those who are not kind to you. Treat others as you want them to treat you. Ask God your Father for whatever you need. Here is how you are to pray to him:

'Our father who art in heaven, hallowed be thy name. Thy kingdom come, thy will be done on earth as it is in heaven. Give us this day our daily bread. And forgive us our trespasses, as we forgive those who trespass against us. And lead us not into temptation, but deliver us from evil.'"

A Storm on the Lake

One evening Jesus said to his apostles, "Let us sail to the other side of the lake." When their boat was out on the water, a storm arose. Winds blew and waves beat against the sides of the little vessel. But Jesus had fallen asleep.

The apostles woke him and cried, "Master, save us or we shall drown!" And Jesus stood and said to the sea, "Peace. Be still." At once the winds fell and the sea grew calm. And Jesus asked the apostles, "Why were you afraid?" And they said to one another, "Who is this Jesus? Even the wind and the waves obey him."

Jesus Feeds the People

A crowd had followed Jesus all day, and in the evening the apostles said, "The people are hungry." And the apostle Philip announced, "A boy is here with five loaves of bread and two fishes, but that is not enough for so many." But Jesus said, "Let the people sit down." After five thousand were seated on the grass, Jesus blessed the loaves and fishes, and the apostles handed them to the crowd. And when everyone had eaten, they picked up what was left, and the food filled twelve baskets. The people were amazed that Jesus had fed so many with so little food.

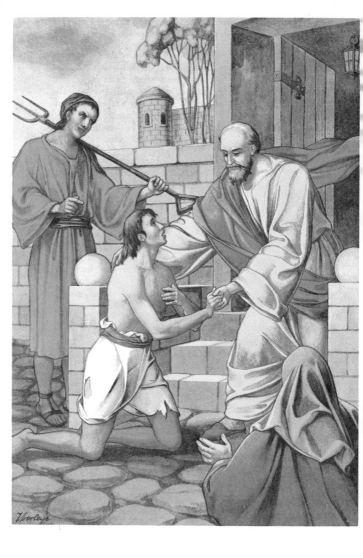

The Loving Father

A young man left home and went to live in a far place where he spent his money foolishly. When it was all gone, he took a job caring for pigs, but the pigs had more to eat than he had, and he said, "The men who work for my father always have enough food. I will go home and ask if I may work for him." He walked along and when his father saw him, he ran to the son and kissed him. And the son said, "Father, I am not worthy to be your son." But the father said to a servant, "Prepare a feast so that we may celebrate my son's return home."

The Story of Zacchaeus

A rich man named Zacchaeus stood in a crowd that waited to see Jesus.

No one liked Zacchaeus, for he made money by collecting taxes from the poor. Because he was short, and tall men stood in front of him, he could not see Jesus, and so he climbed to a high place. But Jesus called to him, "Come down. I want to stay in your house today." The people said, "Why is Jesus going to stay with this wicked man?" But Zacchaeus was sorry for what he had done, and he said, "If I have cheated anyone, I will pay it back, ' and Jesus was pleased with him.

Jesus Cures a Blind Man

When Jesus saw a blind man begging at the side of a road, he put clay on the blind man's eyes and told him to go and wash it off. The man obeyed and at once he was able to see. His parents were amazed, for they knew their son had been born blind and had been that way all his life.

Not long after, Jesus again met the man who had been born blind, and he asked him, "Do you believe in the Son of God?" The man said, "Who is he? Tell me and I will believe in him." Jesus said, "It is I. You are looking at God's Son." And the man knelt down and worshiped him.

The Raising of Lazarus

When Jesus heard that his friend Lazarus had died, he went to visit the dead man's sisters. One of them, Mary, said to Jesus, "If you had been here, Lazarus would not have died."

Jesus said, "Let us go to the cave where he is buried." When they reached it, Jesus said, "Take away the stone that closes the cave." Then he prayed, "Father in heaven, do what I ask you today so that those who are standing here will know it was you who sent me." Then he cried, "Lazarus, come out of the tomb." At once the man who had been dead got up and walked out to his friends.

Jesus Enters Jerusalem

When Jesus was near Jerusalem, two of his friends brought him a young ass, and Jesus sat upon it to ride into the city. Many people threw their coats on the road in front of him, and others cut branches from trees and cast them in his path to show their love for Jesus. Then those who marched before him began to praise God for the wonderful things Jesus had done for them and for all he had taught them.

They shouted:

"Blessed is he who comes as king in the name of the Lord! Hosanna to the son of David! Glory in the highest!"

The Last Supper

On Holy Thursday, Jesus washed the feet of his apostles and then sat down to eat supper with them. During the meal, he took bread and gave it to the apostles and said, "Take this and eat; it is my body." Then he took a cup of wine and said, "Drink this; it is my blood."

And he said to his apostles, "Love one another as I love you. Soon I will leave you to go to my Father. But I will send the Holy Spirit who will live with you and teach you what you need to know."

Then Jesus and the apostles sang a hymn and prayed together.

Jesus is Put to Death

Men in power hated Jesus because he had said he was the Son of God. Now Judas, the apostle, did an evil act. He told the enemies of Jesus where to find him, and on Holy Thursday they arrested him. When the judges asked him if he were truly the Son of God, Jesus would not deny it. Then he was flogged, and soldiers put a crown of thorns on his head because the people had called him their king.

On Good Friday Jesus was taken to Golgotha and nailed to a cross, and there he died. His friends took down his body, wrapped it in a sheet, and buried it in a cave.

The First Easter

On Easter morning, some women went to the tomb where Jesus lay, to put spices on his body. Suddenly they remembered that a heavy stone had been rolled in front of the tomb. One woman said, "Who will roll away the stone for us?" But when they got there it had already been rolled away, and a man in white robes was sitting in the tomb. He said, "Do not be afraid. Jesus has risen from the dead. Tell Peter and the other apostles." As the women ran off, they saw Jesus, and they knelt to adore him. And he said, "Tell the apostles to wait for me in Galilee."

The Apostles See the Risen Jesus

The apostles were indoors when Jesus came to them and said, "Peace be with you." He showed them his wounded hands. But Thomas, one of the apostles, was not there, and when they told him they had seen Jesus, he said, "I do not believe it. If I can put my fingers in his wounds, I will believe he is risen."

Again Jesus came, and when he saw Thomas he said, "Put your fingers into my wounds." But Thomas said, "My Lord and my God." And Jesus said, "You believe because you see me. Blessed are people who do not see me and who believe."

The Ascension

After Jesus rose from the dead, he stayed on earth for forty days, visiting his apostles and talking to them. He said to them, "Go and teach all people what I have taught you. But wait in Jerusalem until I send you the Holy Spirit." After that, Jesus led them to Mount Olivet and blessed them. Then he rose slowly toward the sky until a cloud hid him from sight. As they kept looking up two men in white appeared and said, "Men of Galilee, why do you stand gazing up at the sky? Jesus, who has gone to heaven, will return again."

And the apostles went back to Jerusalem.

The Coming of the Holy Spirit

The apostles, Mary, the mother of Jesus, and their friends prayed and waited for the coming of the Holy Spirit. Then, one day, they heard a sound like the wind, and tongues of fire settled on them. All were filled with the Holy Spirit and they began to speak in many languages. Now visitors from other lands were in Jerusalem, and when the apostles began to speak, the visitors said, "How is it that, no matter what countries we come from, we hear the apostles speaking in our own languages?" The apostles told the story of God's son and great numbers believed in Jesus and became his followers.

THE CATHOLIC CHURCH

When the Spirit entered the hearts
of the apostles, the Church of Jesus
Christ was born. The Spirit-filled
apostles preached to all who were
in Jerusalem for Pentecost.
Thousands listened and believed.
After Pentecost, the visitors went
home with a splendid tale to tell.
The Jesus story spread to distant
lands.

The apostles spread the good
news too. In towns and cities they
preached the glory of Jesus. They
told people of his suffering and
death. They instructed them in his
ways. They shared the miracle of
his resurrection and his promise of

everlasting life. This was a new and wonderful message. It delighted the people to hear it. All who believed were changed. All became more kind, more loving, more like Jesus.

A man named Saul changed the most. Saul didn't like the apostles. He didn't want people to listen to them. He tried to stop their preaching. One day Jesus filled Saul with the Holy Spirit. And Saul became Saint Paul, God's most magnificent preacher. Some people didn't want Paul preaching in their cities. They tried to silence him. They arrested him and beat him and put him in chains. Nothing would stop him. For thirty years Paul continued to spread God's word.

Peter was a great preacher too. Jesus named Peter "Rock." He said, "On this rock I will build my Church." Peter was a leader in the Church. He guided the apostles. He helped them with problems. He answered their questions. The apostles traveled to Rome for meetings because Peter was there.

The Church became very powerful. Some people were jealous. They threatened all who joined the Church. Christians were arrested and punished. Some were killed by angry mobs. Some were ordered not to speak of Jesus. But the Church just became all the more powerful.

Do you know the difference between Church with a big C and

church with a small c? When we say Church with a big C, we mean God's people. When we say chuch with a small c, we mean a building where God's people worship. There are many churches with a small c. There is only one Church with a capital C.

How can all God's people be one Church? Through the one Spirit sent by Jesus. The sacraments bring us the Spirit. Our baptism connects us. The Eucharist joins us to Christians in China or Africa or South America. Every hour of the day, the Eucharist is celebrated somewhere in the world!

We are all part of the Church with a big C. We are the Communion of Saints. We are the

Christians on earth. We are the Christians in heaven. We are the Christians waiting for heaven. We are the Church Jesus founded at Pentecost—and Jesus is with us always.

Best Sellers from The Regina Press

Available from your local dealer or religious book store

America's Leading First Communion Books

1525	**The Marian Children's Mass Book**
1580	**First Steps to Jesus**
1915	**Precious Moments**

Additional Best Sellers

1400	**My First Bible**
1400C	**My First Bible** (CATHOLIC EDITION)
1418	**Guardian Angel Prayer Book**
1419	**My First Prayer Book**
1420	**The Catholic Children's Prayer Book**
1428	**The Children's Book of Saints**
1430	**The Book of Saints**
1519	**The Catholic Children's Bible**
1900	**Precious Moments: My First Book of Prayers**
1905	**Precious Moments: Book of Prayers**

The Little Angel Series

1800	**My First Mass Book**	1806	**The Saints Vol. I**
1801	**The Rosary**	1807	**The Saints Vol. II**
1802	**The Life of Jesus**	1808	**The New Testament**
1803	**The Bible**	1809	**The Sacraments**
1804	**My First Prayer Book**	1810	**The Way of the Cross**
1805	**The Ten Commandments**	1811	**The Christmas Story**

The Regina Press Coloring Books Series

720	**We Go to Mass**	1729	**The Story of Christmas**
721	**The Rosary**	1730	**Heroes of God**
722	**The Saints Vol. I**	1731	**The Ten Commandments/**
723	**The Saints Vol. II**		**The Beatitudes**
725	**The Life of Jesus**	1732	**The Sacraments/**
726	**The Life of Mary**		**The Works of Mercy**
727	**My First Prayer Book**	1733	**The Story of Easter**
728	**The Bible**	1734	**The Way of the Cross**

MRP The Regina Press